J. K.
ROWLING

WORK IT, GIRL

BOSS THE BESTSELLER LIST LIKE

J. K.

Written
by
Caroline
Moss

Illustrated
by
Sinem
Erkas

ROWLING

Frances Lincoln
Children's Books

Chapter 1

An Ordinary Child

· · · · · · · · · · · ·

At the end of July in 1965, in a tiny English village north of Bristol, a baby was born. She was an ordinary baby, by all accounts. She had no magic powers to speak of, at least not yet anyway, and she was not regarded widely as special or unique in any way. But the world would come to know her differently in a few decades time.

That child's name was Joanne Rowling, or, as friends and family called her, Jo. And as a kid Jo loved to tell stories. Even at the young ages of four and five she was telling fantasy stories to her younger sister Dianne (who never much wanted to hear them). By the time Jo started Kindergarten, she had already earned herself a reputation in the family for being the storyteller and performer. She loved hearing stories, too—she was a keen reader and would often beg her parents to read her books until she could lock herself away with her favorite titles on her own.

She was always reading, and everyone noticed her nose buried in her books. Her mom also loved books and was delighted by her daughter's interest, nurturing it as much as she could. It was a way the two could connect and find common ground.

When she was a little older, Jo's great-aunt started to notice her young niece's passion for language arts and gifted her a copy of a book called *Hons and Rebels* by a woman named Jessica Mitford. Jo loved it so much, she became obsessed with all of her books and writing. Not able to get enough of the words and stories jumping out at her from the page, Jessica was her "heroine" and Jo was determined to follow her newest, most real dream: She wanted to write stories people would read. She wanted to be like Jessica Mitford, and inspire others to tell their stories or the ones living in their heads.

Joanne Rowling knew, for sure, that she wanted to become a real-life author.

EVENTUALLY, HER OTHER FAMILY MEMBERS STARTED TO SEE THAT THE YOUNG GIRL HAD CAUGHT A LITERARY BUG OF SORTS.

"IT MATTERS NOT WHAT SOMEONE IS BORN,
BUT WHAT THEY GROW TO BE."

— J. K. Rowling

Chapter 2

The Teen who Lived

It was not a perfect childhood for Jo. When she was only 15, her mother Anne was diagnosed with a muscular illness called MS. The shocking diagnosis stunned Jo and the rest of her family. All of a sudden, everything Jo had come to rely on was falling out from underneath her, and she found herself holding tight to the time she shared with her mother. The illness took over Anne's life and she became a shell of her former self. It was hard for her to do simple things like take a bath or help Jo set the table for dinner. Jo would often curl up with her mother in bed and read books, even though Anne was too weak to be fully present in those moments.

Life was hard—her mother was unable to do many things and her illness took up the emotional energy of her daughters and husband. With one parent often unavailable, Jo was left to spend time mostly with her father, whom she did not get along with. She was not a happy young woman, as she was dealing with so much more than the average teenager does. In a way, Anne's illness forced Jo to be a grown-up far before she was prepared to. Sometimes, she wished she was just like other normal teenagers who only had to worry about school dances and history exams.

Jo attended primary and secondary school in the U.K., meeting people who would later serve as references for some of her most beloved book characters—but more on them later! Right now, Jo was known for being a mediocre student, but her teachers do remember that she was bright, especially when it came to writing and literature.

Have you ever heard the phrase "living up to your potential"? It means that others around you might see something in you that you are having a hard time seeing yourself. It may mean that others believe you could be working harder to achieve big goals but that you may be holding yourself back. This was classic Joanne Rowling, as her educators remember. Whether it was because of issues at home or something else, Jo had a promise inside of her that she was, her teachers believed, not living up to.

They believed she was meant for big things, but also knew that big things required big work, and Jo wasn't super interested in putting in the work at the time.

Jo became desperate to fit in at school, and found herself to be a little bit of a hippie who spent a lot of time playing guitar in her bedroom. While she never abandoned her love of storytelling and books, she found music to be a great way for her to channel energy and emotion, especially when things at home weren't

going so well: music got her through the tough times. But she never truly became very engaged with her school work, which made her teachers and professors scratch their heads in wonder.

WHY WON'T JO JUST DO THE WORK?

Jo still really wanted to be a writer but boy, oh boy, she did not want to do the work to become one. Writing papers for school was a headache. Jo was starting to wonder if she was really destined for a life of storytelling. But what she didn't know was that being able to write the stories she created in her own mind would help unlock all of that unused potential inside of her.

By the time Jo became a senior in high school, she had decided her heart was set on attending the prestigious Oxford University. But Oxford was a very competitive school, and only accepted the top students from all over the world. Jo was hopeful admissions counselors would see her bright and shiny potential through some of her dismal grades and held onto hope as the weeks and months passed after submitting her application. She dreamed of her life at Oxford, the stories she would write and the things she would learn if. If she got in, she promised herself that she would study very hard and achieve high marks.

Finally, an envelope arrived from Oxford. Jo held it in her hand. *This is my future!* She thought. She ran up to her bedroom and tore the envelope open, flopping on her bed.

"Thank you for your application to Oxford University," the letter read. "We regret to inform you have not been accepted."

Jo was totally crushed. She thought her future was slipping away from her and she started to kick herself for not doing a better job of fulfilling her potential in high school. Her grades throughout school were not impressive enough to be let in, and Jo was full of regret that she had let some of her work slip over the years.

But all was not lost. Jo attended another great school— the University of Exeter—where she studied French and classics. (Classics is the study of Greek and Roman culture.) She truly loved the work, going to class, and learning from her professors. She found herself paying attention and studying hard for good marks—keeping that same promise she made to herself back when she was pining for Oxford. Maybe she could become a real writer like Jessica Mitford ...

"**YOU'VE GOT TO** BE PREPARED FOR HITTING WRONG NOTES OCCASIONALLY, OR QUITE A LOT.

THAT'S JUST PART OF THE LEARNING PROCESS.

AND READ A LOT.

READING

A LOT

REALLY

HELPS.

 **READ**

 **ANYTHING**

 **YOU**

 **CAN**

 **GET**

YOUR

 **HANDS**

 **ON."**

— J. K. Rowling

Chapter 3

The Pity Party is Over

• • • • • • • • • • •

What is a writer? A writer, simply, is someone who writes. Maybe you are a writer, or you know a writer. But to be a full-time published author means that your writing earns enough money to help you pay for all of the necessities required for you to live. It's a job, just like being a doctor, or a bus driver, or a teacher.

Jo wanted to be an author, but she didn't realize how stressful the life of a full-time writer would be—or how hard it would be to achieve the opportunity to write, and only write, instead of having another paying job to supplement the bills.

She left university, diploma in hand, ready to achieve her dreams of becoming an author—one who told stories and changed the world. How hard could it be?

Answer: Hard! Writing did not earn Jo any money, and it wouldn't until she could get steady work publishing her work. So, she had to find another job, any job, to help pay the bills.

Jo scanned the "wanted" ads for anything that could help keep her afloat. She eventually found a job as a researcher and a secretary for Amnesty International in London. This was not a writing job, she would grumble. It wasn't even close. And

AMNESTY INTERN for a SECRETARY

Call for an interview

it wasn't even nearby. Jo would often be commuting for hours and hours to get to work. If the trains broke down, or were very busy, she'd spend nearly the same time getting to work as she did *at* work. It was enough to make a person scream! But she really found herself enjoying Amnesty. The organization is the world's largest human rights organization, and Jo found the people who worked for it to be nice and motivating. But the commute was still terrible, and she was still not a writer.

Jo felt sorry for herself for a little while. If you've ever had something in your life go wrong, you might have sat around pitying yourself, too. Jo got bored of moping. Once she was done spending her energy complaining in her head, she started dreaming up stories like the ones she had created as a little girl …

"IF SOMEONE ASKED FOR MY RECIPE FOR HAPPINESS, STEP ONE WOULD BE FINDING OUT WHAT YOU LOVE DOING MOST IN THE WORLD ...

AND STEP TWO WOULD BE FINDING SOMEONE TO PAY YOU TO DO IT."
— J. K. Rowling

Chapter 4

I Have an Idea

· · · · · · · · · · ·

The train was stalled yet again, but at least Jo had a seat. She started to daydream about her newest idea, a fantasy story about a boy wizard. But in the beginning, he doesn't know he's a wizard. He just thinks he's a normal boy. Then he finds out the truth, and adventure unfolds...

Was this interesting? Jo thought. She looked around the crowded train at the other commuters making their way into London. Would any of them read a story about a wizard? Probably not. They all looked very serious.

But Jo couldn't get the little boy

named Harry out of her head. He was taking up her entire brain! She kept thinking about what his life would be like, where he would go to school, and who his friends would be. She was yearning to put this all on paper. She tapped her foot impatiently all day at work and looked at the clock. Finally, it was time to go home. She grabbed a few pieces of paper and a pen and tucked them into her bag on the way out of the office.

She couldn't wait to get to the train. The story was exploding from her brain onto the page. She couldn't write fast enough to get everything down.

She didn't tell anyone about her story for a long time. Jo didn't know if anyone would get it, and she was so excited about her idea that she worried if just one person told her it was stupid, she would be so devastated she'd give up on writing it. So, each day she went to work and each day she wrote diligently, tucking pages into her bag when the train would pull into her stop at night. She didn't even tell her boyfriend about it.

Jo really thought she had something good on her hands, but she was terrified of finding out if others disagreed with her. If you have ever been afraid of being

wrong, you know how this feels.

At the same time, Jo's mother was still sick, and later that year, sadly died. Jo was torn apart. She had never even told her mother about her idea—and her mother would have been so proud of her. She would have loved the story. She would have been so excited. All of a sudden, her book became even more three-dimensional than intended. It was a diary of sorts, a way for Jo to channel all of her feelings about the death of her mother through her characters and her stories.

SHE WROTE, AND WROTE, AND WROTE.

ANYTHING'S POSSIBLE IF YOU'VE GOT ENOUGH NERVE

— J. K. Rowling

Chapter 5

The World is her Oyster

· · · · · · · · · · · ·

Some days all Jo wanted to do was write. Others, she avoided it like a plague. Sometimes she'd even go weeks without touching her project. But it was always on her mind, even though her job and her relationship with her boyfriend took up a lot of her time (not to mention the train rides to and from the office). Soon, Jo realized she would have to make big changes in order to take her book seriously. So she made two huge decisions: she broke up with her boyfriend and left her job. She wanted a brand new start. She had pages upon pages of a young wizard's adventures written, and there were still so many left to write. The characters leapt off the paper with every page she wrote. There were so many stories left to tell about this boy and his friends! She could see them so clearly. But they still remained a big secret to the world around her.

While looking for a job, she noticed the weather outside. Gloomy and gray, it seemed that London was nearly always sort of sad. Without a boyfriend, Jo was truly independent, and only had to fend for herself. So why was she only looking for a job in London? That made her think ...

Why not dream bigger, and expand the job search?

Almost immediately, she came across a job advert looking for English-speaking teachers to move to Porto, a beautiful city in Portugal. She eagerly applied and was delighted when she found out she was accepted. What a different feeling than the day she got the rejection letter from Oxford. She taught at night, so she spent her days writing about—you guessed it—the young wizard and his best friends, and all of their wild adventures in a magical world that existed only in her imagination.

Jo knew in her bones she was going to be an author. She could feel it more than ever. Every chapter she wrote made her more excited about the world she was creating in her stories. Who would read these stories? Would they love them? Would they be inspired by them? She felt the answer was "yes". And so she wrote and wrote and wrote.

While she was teaching, she met a man named Jorge who she soon married, and in July of 1993 they had a daughter named Jessica (named after Jo's favorite author, Jessica Mitford)! Life could not have been better.

But as she soon learned, good things—and bad things—always change. Nothing stays the same. Life is a series of ups and downs, good moods and not-so-good moods, great successes and sometimes great disappointments. Unfortunately, a few months after Jessica was born, Jo and her husband Jorge separated. They did not get along anymore and it didn't make sense to stay together. But the divorce left Jo and Jessica to fend for themselves, which was difficult.

Jo ended up making a tough decision. She moved to Scotland with Jessica, where she had a sister who could support them. Jo didn't even have a winter coat, but she brought a suitcase full of Jessica's belongings, and three chapters of a book about a little boy who discovers he's a wizard.

Jo had a book to write, and she wouldn't let any part of life get in the way of the magic.

"THE KNOWLEDGE THAT YOU HAVE EMERGED WISER AND STRONGER FROM SETBACKS MEANS THAT YOU ARE, EVER AFTER,

SECURE IN YOUR ABILITY TO SURVIVE."

— J. K. Rowling

Chapter 6

F is for Failure?
Or F is for Future?

• • • • • • • • • • • •

Despite her dream, Jo felt a familiar feeling. She felt as if the floor was pulled out from under her again, like when she found out her beloved mom was very ill. She felt like she was not good enough like when she was reading the rejection letter from Oxford. It felt like failure. She was depressed. She was lonely. She was exhausted. She thought her life was over. And she had very little money to her name. Raising a child was expensive, both in time and in money, so she barely got a chance to keep writing her story. As a single mother, she just could not find the time.

Jo thought she could kiss goodbye to being the next Jessica Mitford. Now she had to work almost twice as hard in a brand new place to keep her and her daughter afloat. She saw no way out, no light at the end of the tunnel. Every day was the same dark and dreary day. Even her daughter, who she loved dearly and fiercely, was not bringing her the happiness she needed and in turn, Jo felt she was not a good parent.

Often, writers take their own experiences in life and turn them into the stories on their pages. This dark time in Jo's life served its purpose in her books. If she had only had sunny days, she may not have been able to write a world that explored both the darkness and the light of living.

Jo ended up applying for benefits from the government, which was helpful, but made her feel "as poor as it is possible to be in modern Britain, without being homeless." She did not want Jessica to grow up feeling any different than the rest of the kids around them, which motivated her to pick herself up and carry on.

Jo pulled out that suitcase she had taken back to Britain from Portugal and dusted it off before popping it open. There it was—her story. The story of a little boy named Harry Potter, who lives under a staircase in the house of a mean aunt and uncle, and who quickly finds out he's a wizard. She loved this story. Jo sighed. She knew what she had to do.

From that day on, Jo focused on her writing in the name of her daughter. She wrote as much as she could, as quickly as she could. She lined up her writing schedule with her daughter's naps.

THE STORY OF HARRY POTTER WOULD LIVE ON.

And Jessica was a terrible sleeper.

But did Jo give up? No. She found a way to make it work. After taking Jessica on long walks, Jo found that her daughter totally and completely zonked out—for a while. Jo would steer the carriage into a bustling café and write while her daughter slept soundly.

Her time to write was limited. After all, babies don't sleep for that long. So Jo would steal 20 minutes, 30 minutes here and there and lose herself in the story. She was fully immersed in the world of wizardry and friendship.

As she sipped her cup of coffee, Jo would plan out as much of her stories as she could. She liked being organized and knowing what would come next, so creating character maps and family trees was crucial. She wanted to create three-dimensional people on paper. It was a lot of work, but it was necessary work for Jo's process.

Though she loved her time with her daughter when she was awake, there was a peace that came over her when she was able to focus on writing while sitting next to her sleepy baby. She knew big things were ahead for Harry—and for herself and Jessica.

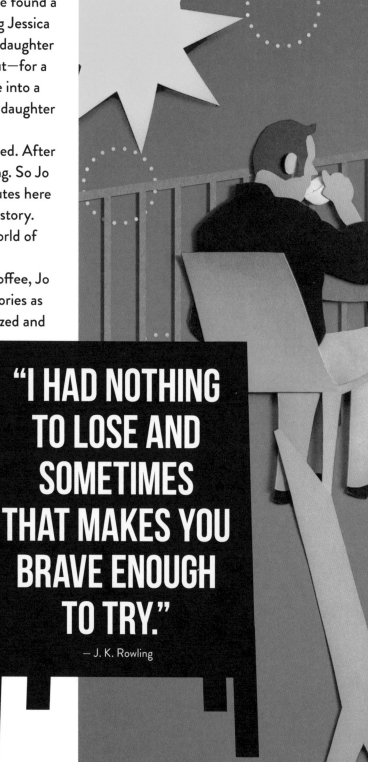

"I HAD NOTHING TO LOSE AND SOMETIMES THAT MAKES YOU BRAVE ENOUGH TO TRY."

— J. K. Rowling

Harry Potter and the Big Fat . . .

"NO!

"NO"

"NO"

"NO"

"NO"

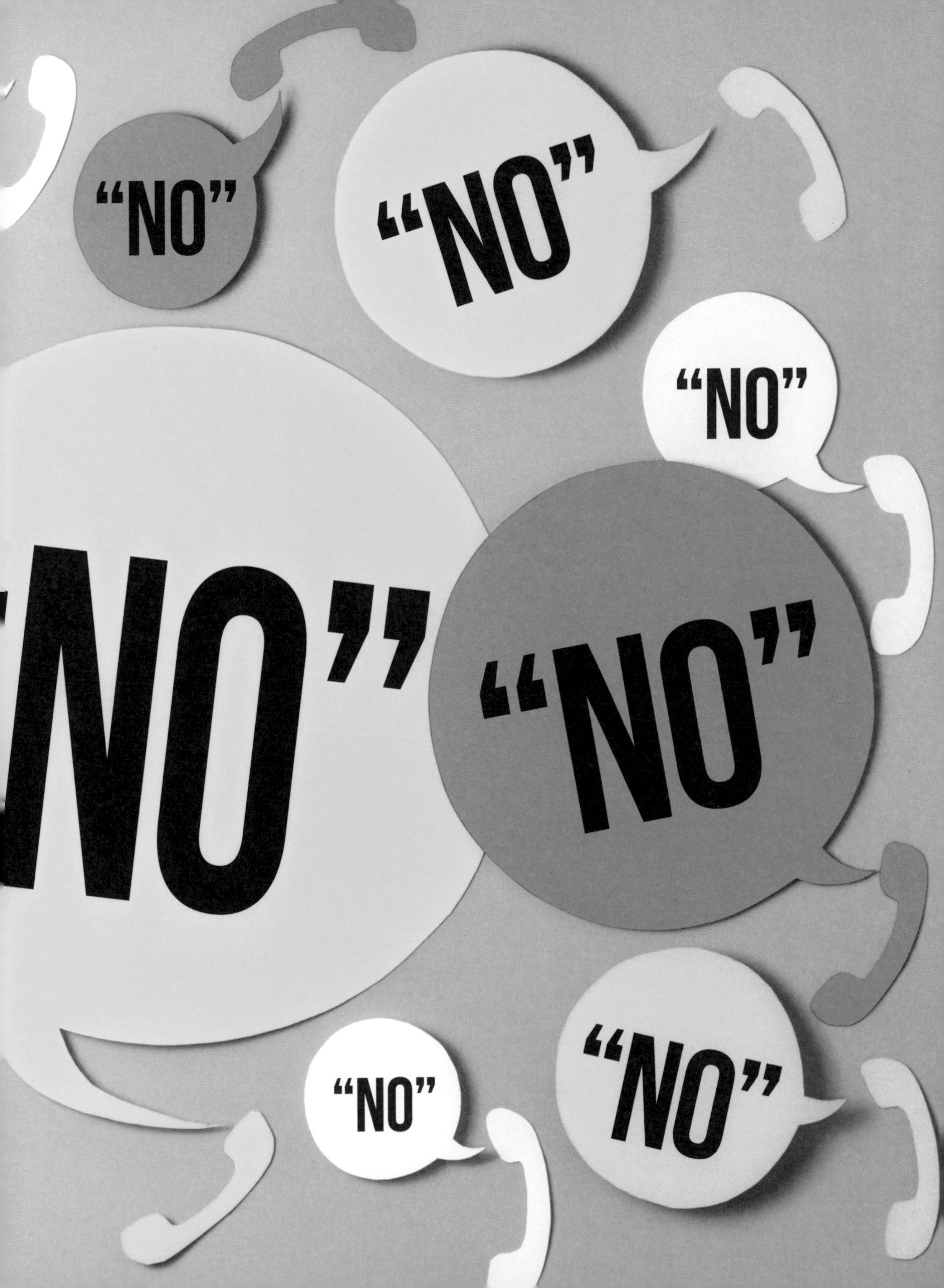
"NO"
"NO"
"NO"
"NO"
"NO"
"NO"
"NO"

In 1995, after logging many hours in that café next to her sleepy baby daughter, Jo finally finished what we would later know as *Harry Potter and the Philosopher's Stone*. As she finished the last sentence and closed the manuscript, she felt a surge of nerves and excitement. She truly believed in her book and she knew with absolute certainty others would feel the same way.

Now all she had to do was find a publisher to buy it. How hard could that be? Jo packed up the book to bring it to publishers. One by one, each publisher wrote back with their answer.

"No thank you," said one.

"This isn't really for us," said another.

"We're not accepting new material at this time," said another.

Twelve publishing houses said no. Jo was crushed twelve times. She thought about how broke she was. She thought about her young daughter, who was growing bigger and bigger every day and had so many needs Jo simply could not afford to meet. She was getting nervous.

Then, one rainy night in London, the manuscript landed in the hands of a man named Barry Cunningham at Bloomsbury. He read it once, then again. He loved the writing but he knew he needed the intended audience to get it as well. Wizards? Hagrid? Muggles? The Mirror of Erised? He knew someone who could help.

He got on the train home that evening with the manuscript in his briefcase. When he walked in the door to his house he was greeted by his young daughter, Alice.

"I have something I want you to read." He kneeled down and took out the book from his briefcase. "Here's chapter one. Read it, and then tell me what you think."

Alice grabbed the papers and disappeared into her room.

The next morning, Barry had to tear the manuscript off Alice. She loved it! And so did the whole team at Bloomsbury. Barry was thrilled he'd got it right, and quickly called Jo to share the news.

> "A LITTLE GIRL NAMED ALICE APPROVES, SO WE'RE GOING TO MOVE FORWARD WITH YOUR BOOK," HE TOLD JO. "BUT DON'T QUIT YOUR DAY JOB. THERE JUST ISN'T A LOT OF MONEY IN CHILDREN'S BOOK PUBLISHING I'M AFRAID."

Jo couldn't believe it. All of a sudden a million memories flashed into her mind. She thought of the long train rides to work, and the day she came up with the idea for her story. She thought of her screaming daughter, who never wanted to nap. She thought about the long hours at the cafe, the days where she could barely afford milk and bread. She thought about how proud her mom would be of her.

She had found a publisher. And she knew deep down inside she had a big hit on her hands. Would she be right? Jo still trusted her gut.

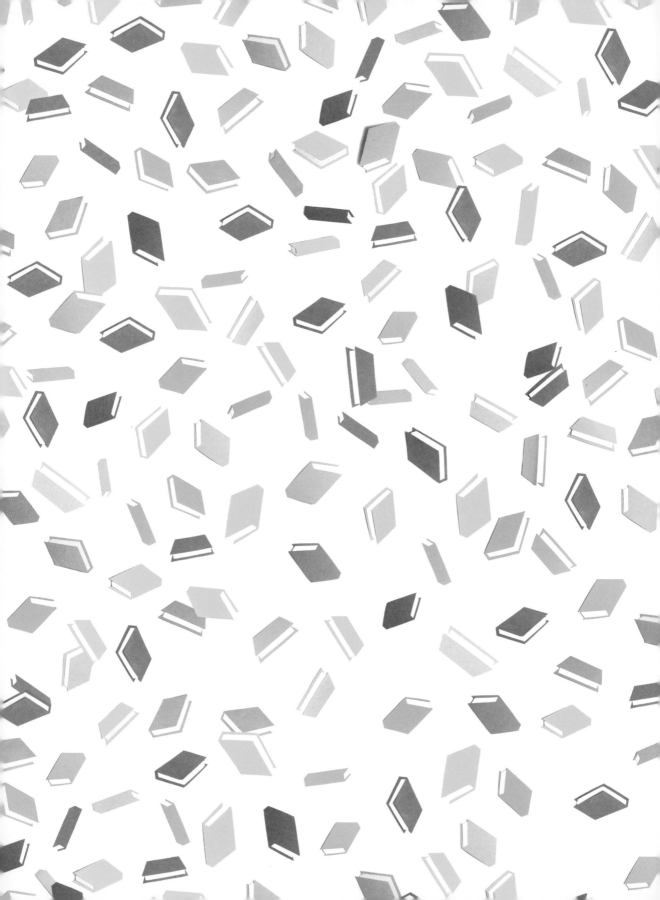

"I WASN'T GOING TO GIVE UP UNTIL EVERY SINGLE PUBLISHER TURNED ME DOWN, BUT I OFTEN FEARED THAT WOULD HAPPEN."

— J. K. Rowling

Chapter 8

A HIT.

· · · · · · · · · · · ·

It wasn't overnight, but there's a reason you, reader, are reading this book right now. You know who Harry Potter is. You've read the books or maybe seen the movies. All of that exists because Jo, a single mother with barely any income, did not give up on her dream to be an author. And she never stopped trusting the voice inside that told her she had a great story just waiting to be read.

Jo could never have guessed just how big *Harry Potter* would become.

In the beginning, the first book was sold to Bloomsbury for a modest "don't-quit-your-job" fee of around £2,000. That might seem like a lot at first, but it wouldn't be enough to support Jo and Jessica for longer than a month or so. The publishing house ran the numbers and decided they would print one thousand copies of the book. If it was selling well, they figured, they could always print more. The publisher also made the decision to change Jo's name to a "pen name"—J. K. Rowling.

The reasoning behind one of the most famous names in fiction was short-sighted. They believed *Harry Potter* would be a "book for boys" and so they thought Jo should go by a more "male-sounding" name. We all now know that's baloney! But J. K. Rowling was the name printed on the books when it debuted in June of 1997. Of the thousand copies the publishing company ordered, only 500 of them were available for sale, with the other half going to libraries. Barry Cunningham hoped that word-of-mouth would spread and demand would go up for Bloomsbury to order more copies.

Jo waited nervously. Would her book make a splash? Big books by big authors usually got lots of attention. There would be adverts on buses and billboards. Sometimes even television appearances or commercials. Big signs at bookstores. But no one knew who J. K. Rowling was. So would they care about *Harry Potter*?

On the day the first review was published, Jo held her breath and squeezed her eyes shut. She took a few deep inhales, squinted her eyes open, and began to read.

"I have yet to find a child who can put it down," raved The Herald. Notice that they wrote the word "child" and not "boy"! Jo gasped and then started to laugh gleefully. *Harry Potter* was for all children, and people were starting to take notice.

The reviews poured in.

All of Britain was buzzing about this new book. In 1997 *Harry Potter* was introduced to editors at Scholastic in the United States, who quickly scooped the book rights up for $105,000! Jo was in shock. But it was still peanuts compared to what would come next.

Harry Potter and the Philosopher's Stone (the United States version swaps in Sorcerer for Philosopher, a change Jo later said she regretted making) had sold over 300,000 copies by 1999 and won a National Book Award. American kids were clamoring for more wizardry, too.

Harry Potter fever had hit. Four years in a row, a new Harry Potter book debuted each summer. Bookstores would open at midnight to hundreds of people waiting in line to buy the new book. Some came dressed up. Some went home right away with their new book and didn't stop reading until they turned the last page at eight o'clock in the morning.

In 2003, the series published its fifth instalment.

Let's talk numbers a little bit. Remember those thousand copies of the first book, the ones that would serve as a "test" for whether *Harry Potter* would be successful? They were now considered rare, with people willing to pay thousands and thousands of dollars to get their hands on a copy.

The books would break records left and right, only to be broken again once the following book would come out. For *Harry Potter and the Goblet of Fire*, 9,000 mail trucks were used solely to deliver the book in the United States!

Jo did not need a day job. This was her whole life. She was writing as fast as she could!

By 2007, the seven-book saga of Harry Potter was complete. Would all of this have happened if Jo had given up on her dream? Absolutely not.

"YOU CONTROL YOUR OWN LIFE. YOUR OWN WILL IS EXTREMELY POWERFUL."

— J. K. Rowling

Chapter 9

From Rags to "Richest"

· · · · · · · · · · · ·

Jo, or J. K. Rowling, was now one of the world's most successful authors ... ever. Her books have sold over 500 million copies worldwide, been adapted into films, and have even given way to a Harry Potter-themed amusement park!

Her life completely transformed because she continued to write even when she had so many other things to think and worry about.

J. K. Rowling became a household name, and served as an inspiring story to others. Details about her life before the smash success of the Harry Potter books started to emerge. Hers was a story for every young student who struggled to truly find her place. For every child whose home life was tumultuous at a young age and forced them to adapt. For every high school senior who had a dream of higher education but was cut short by a rejection letter. For every entry-level worker who wasn't working their dream career. Now people knew Jo had written this amazing series, while also living off state benefits and caring for her young daughter as a single parent. Her story proved naysayers wrong.

In 2008, Jo was asked to speak at the prestigious Harvard University graduation ceremony as a keynote speaker. In the days leading up to giving her speech she was so nervous with anticipation she couldn't eat anything.

She wasn't a diligent college student when she was their age, so why would these kids, graduating from the most prestigious Ivy League university in America, want to listen to her? She started to have doubts.

But she did it anyway. On a spring day in May, Jo stood in front of college graduates and told them her story. She told them about how she slacked off a lot in school and how her teachers never thought she was living up to her potential. She talked about wanting to be a writer, and how she felt like a failure when her marriage ended and she had to fill out the paperwork to receive financial help from the government.

Jo looked out onto the lawn full of students and their families and guests and took a deep breath.

"So why do I talk about the benefits of failure?" she spoke out. "Simply because failure meant a stripping away of the inessential. I stopped pretending to myself that I was anything other than what I was, and began to direct all my

energy into finishing the only work that mattered to me."

She looked out again on the lawn. They seemed to really be listening to what she was saying. She said that, looking back, she was happy she didn't seem to find her niche anywhere else because it forced her to hone in on her writing passion. She talked about how the Harvard students, being some of the brightest in the nation, may not have a ton of experience with failure, but reminded them that failure happens to everyone at some point along their journey.

"I WOULD TELL MY 21-YEAR-OLD SELF THAT PERSONAL HAPPINESS LIES IN KNOWING THAT LIFE IS NOT A CHECKLIST …" SHE TOLD THE STUDENTS. "YOUR QUALIFICATIONS ARE NOT YOUR LIFE … LIFE IS DIFFICULT, AND COMPLICATED, AND BEYOND ANYONE'S TOTAL CONTROL."

— Seneca

"AS IS A TALE, SO IS LIFE: NOT HOW LONG IT IS, BUT HOW GOOD IT IS, IS WHAT MATTERS."

Looking Back

· · · · · · · · · · ·

J. K. Rowling is not the most famous writer in the world because she was born into a rich and famous family, or went to the best college in the world, or was the best student in the world.

But.

She knew she loved to write, and she honored that passion every day. She did not write thinking, "I am going to write the book that makes me a billion dollars." She wrote because she had a story in her head that she desperately needed to tell. She honored her imagination and worked hard to become great at her craft.

She took chances, and got rejected.

And then she took more chances.

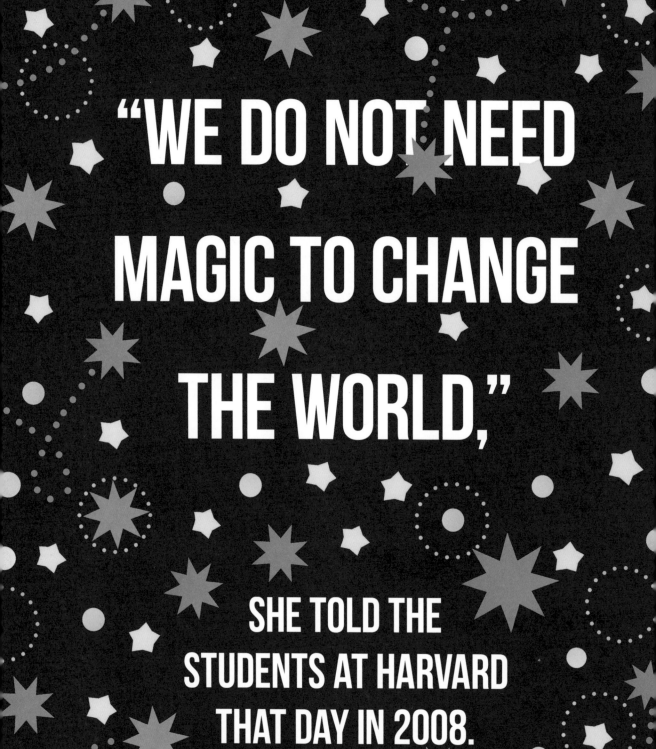

"WE DO NOT NEED MAGIC TO CHANGE THE WORLD,"

SHE TOLD THE STUDENTS AT HARVARD THAT DAY IN 2008.

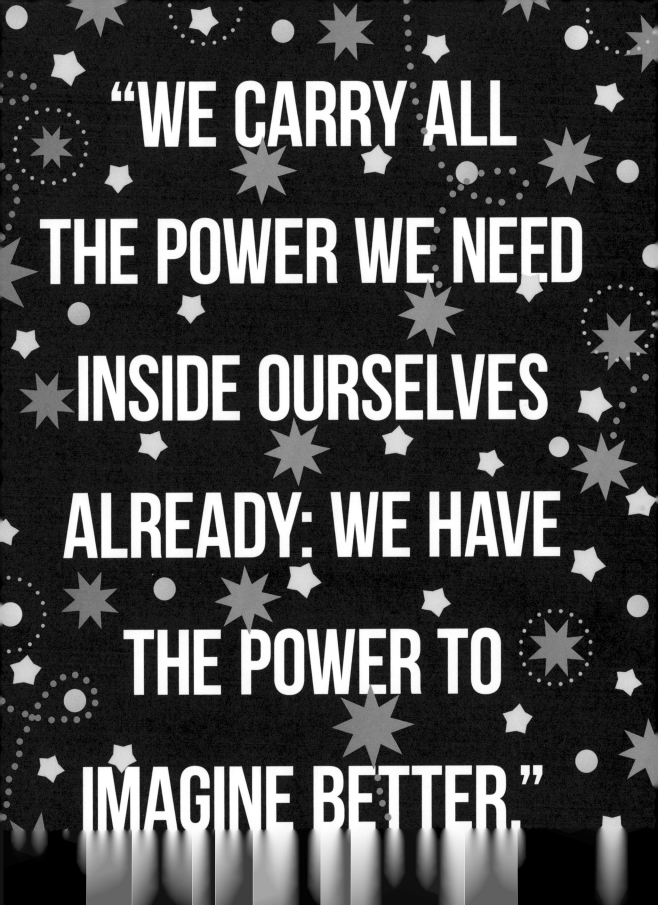

"WE CARRY ALL THE POWER WE NEED INSIDE OURSELVES ALREADY: WE HAVE THE POWER TO IMAGINE BETTER."

Chapter 10

Giving Back

• • • • • • • • • • •

Joanne Rowling knows that she has worked hard to get to where she is. She knows it wasn't so long ago that she was down on her luck, forced to make hard choices for herself and her daughter in order to inch closer to her dream of being an author. She also knows she is lucky; that there are many women just like her who may never achieve the same success she has.

So she makes sure she gives back, in big ways and in small.

In 2012, she was bumped off the Forbes' billionaires list for a pretty good reason—she was no longer a billionaire. Why? She gave enough of her fortune away to good causes. Isn't that inspiring?

But it's not just about money. Jo donates her time and her platform as well, speaking out for causes that she cares about like poverty and children's literacy. She speaks out against intolerance and hate. She even wrote three books whose profits went directly to various causes.

Throughout her life, Jo always felt that one person was missing out on watching her grow into one of the most accomplished authors of her time. Her mother, Anne. But in 2010, she used $8.5 million dollars to open the Anne Rowling Neurology Clinic in her name. It was a way she could honor her mother and also give back to others going through what Anne experienced.

So much of Jo's success can be credited back to her true love of writing, while the success and money was secondary. It's why she continues to write even though her fortune would allow her to never lift a finger again, and it's why she's found so much success in the first place.

> "YOU HAVE A MORAL RESPONSIBILITY WHEN YOU'VE BEEN GIVEN FAR MORE THAN YOU NEED, TO DO WISE THINGS WITH IT AND GIVE INTELLIGENTLY," SHE HAS SAID IN INTERVIEWS.

Jo accomplished something so many
aspiring writers dream of doing: she
wrote a book that changed the lives of
millions of people. Her words—the ones
that were inspired by hard days and good

days, sunny moments and not-so-sunny
moments—all turned into a creative story
that adults and children fell in love with.
It made all of those difficult days worth
living through in the end.

"WHATEVER

MONEY YOU MIGHT HAVE,

SELF-WORTH

REALLY LIES

in Finding Out

What You Do
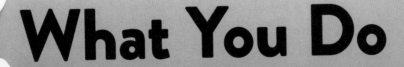

BEST."

— J. K. Rowling

Write to your heart's content, like J. K. Rowling!

10 key lessons from J. K. Rowling's life

1 **Good writing starts with good reading!**
Jo discovered her love for reading early on in her life, which then gave her the skills she needed to start working on telling her own stories. Being a good writer means you have to also read a lot. A librarian or teacher can help you discover books you love.

2 **If you work hard now, it will pay off later.**
Remember how Jo really wanted to go to Oxford, the prestigious university? Unfortunately, her grades just didn't make the cut, even though she so desperately wanted to attend. If you work hard now, you will have more opportunities in the future to do the things you want to do!

3 **Not every job is going to be your dream job.**
Before she was able to support herself with her writing, Jo had lots of jobs that she wouldn't consider her "dream job." But having steady work helped her support her writing hobby so that one day she could try to make it her full-time job.

4 **Trust your ideas!**
If you have a great idea, run with it! Jo dreamed up Harry Potter's world on a train ride. She started to write. She did not worry what people were going to think of her story until much later. She did not try to write a bestselling book in one day. But she trusted her gut and worked at it until she could get others to see her vision, too.

5 **You are not a tree! If you want to change directions, you can.**
The world is a big, beautiful place, and there is no one way to lead
a meaningful life. You can explore lots of different paths to see
where you belong.

6 **Failure is an opportunity.**
Everyone fails! Everyone! Failure helps you grow and learn.
Failure helps shape who you will ultimately become.
Welcome and accept failure instead of fearing it,
and you will have succeeded.

7 **If you believe in yourself, it's easier for others to believe in you.**
You have to be your biggest fan first.

8 **Ride your momentum.**
It would have been easy for Jo to sign off after writing *Harry
Potter and the Philospher's Stone*. Instead, she kept writing,
and writing, and writing, until she created a world that captured
people's imaginations. One hit book helped her get another
and another. She grabbed opportunity by the horns.

9 **Never get too big for your britches.**
Stay humble! It helps others relate to you and your work.
J. K. Rowling is the biggest author alive, but she makes you
feel like you could be her friend. Wouldn't it be nice if
everyone had this attitude?

10 **Give back!**
Appreciate how lucky you are and share that luck with those less
fortunate. Even if you are not a billionaire or a famous celebrity,
there is always someone in the world who has less than you do.

Grab a sheet of paper, and a pencil, and answer these questions!

J. K. Rowling dreamed up lots of stories.
Do you have any stories you're dreaming of telling?
What are they?

• • • • • • • • • • •

This book taught us that failure can be a good thing!
Have you ever "failed" at something and learned a good
lesson, or used your failure to help you succeed later?
Tell us about it!

• • • • • • • • • • •

If you had a million dollars to give back,
what would you do with it?

• • • • • • • • • • •

If you were asked to speak in front of a crowd,
what message would you share with those listening?

Further reading

· · · · · · · · · · ·

Check out these other great books and resources by J. K. Rowling.
You can also read about and help the charities she supports, listed below.

Fiction
The Harry Potter series by J. K. Rowling:
Harry Potter and the Philosopher's Stone
Harry Potter and the Chamber of Secrets
Harry Potter and the Prisoner of Azkaban
Harry Potter and the Goblet of Fire
Harry Potter and the Order of the Phoenix
Harry Potter and the Half-Blood Prince
Harry Potter and the Deathly Hallows
Fantastic Beasts and Where to Find Them by J. K. Rowling

Non-fiction
Very Good Lives by J. K. Rowling

Screenplays
Harry Potter and the Cursed Child by J. K. Rowling, John Tiffany and Jack Thorne

Advanced Reading
The Cuckoo's Calling by J. K. Rowling, writing as Robert Galbraith

Online
Pottermore

Charities
Lumos
Gingerbread
The Anne Rowling Regenerative Neurology Clinic

To Ella, whose wild imagination will help build a world all of us will want to live in.—C.M.

Work It, Girl J. K. Rowling © 2019 Quarto Publishing plc.
Text © 2019 Caroline Moss. Illustrations © 2019 Sinem Erkas.

First Published in 2019 by Frances Lincoln Children's Books, an imprint of The Quarto Group.

400 First Avenue North, Suite 400, Minneapolis, MN 55401, USA.

T (612) 344-8100 F (612) 344-8692 www.QuartoKnows.com

ISBN 978-1-78603-469-4

The illustrations were created in paper. Set in Brandon Grotesque and Bebas Neue.

Published by Rachel Williams. Designed by Sinem Erkas.
Paper Modelling by Sinem Erkas and Christopher Noulton.
Paper assistance by Tijen Erkas.
Edited by Katy Flint. Production by Jenny Cundill.

Manufactured in China CC062019
9 8 7 6 5 4 3

Photo credits p20: Children's writer J. K. Rowling at King's Cross station, 1999 © Denis Jones via REX/Shutterstock; p42, top: Harry Potter rare first edition auction, 2003 © Getty Images; p42, bottom: J. K. Rowling reads from Harry Potter book, 2005 © Christopher Furlong via Getty Images.